THE STORY OF

BENJAMIN FRANKLIN,
Amazing American

BY MARGARET DAVIDSON

ILLUSTRATED BY JOHN SPEIRS

═══════ THE STORY OF ═══════

BENJAMIN FRANKLIN,
Amazing American

BY MARGARET DAVIDSON

ILLUSTRATED BY JOHN SPEIRS

A YEARLING BOOK

ABOUT THIS BOOK

The events described in this book are true. They have been carefully researched and excerpted from authentic autobiographies, writings, and commentaries. No part of this biography has been fictionalized.

To learn more about Benjamin Franklin, ask your librarian to recommend other fine books you might read.

*Especially for Terry Van Tell,
a wonderful friend*

Published by
Dell Publishing Co., a division of
The Bantam Doubleday Dell
Publishing Group, Inc.
1 Dag Hammarskjold Plaza
New York, NY 10017

Yearling ® TM 913705, Dell Publishing Co., a division of
The Bantam Doubleday Dell
Publishing Group, Inc.

ISBN: 0-440-40021-X

Published by arrangement with Parachute Press, Inc.
Printed in the United States of America
March 1988

10 9 8 7 6 5 4 3 2 1

CW

Ben Writes a Letter

IT WAS ALMOST AN HOUR BEFORE DAWN, and the city of Boston was dark and still. In all the town no one was stirring . . . except for a boy named Ben. He slipped through the streets until he came to a certain shop. He looked both ways. He stooped and shoved a piece of paper under the door. Then he turned and hurried away.

But he was back a few hours later—for that was where he worked. It was a print shop, and it belonged to Ben's older brother James. James also published a newspaper called the *New England Courant*.

That afternoon several of James's friends stopped by for a visit. And James showed them the paper. It was an article signed Silence Dogood. "What do you think of this?" he asked.

"I'll tell you one thing," someone commented. "Whoever wrote this has a truly active and inventive mind."

Ben's Big Ideas

ACTIVE AND INVENTIVE—THOSE WERE good words to describe Benjamin Franklin, even as a small boy.

Ben was born in Boston on a cold and snowy day in January of 1706. He had sixteen brothers and sisters. Thirteen of them lived to grow up. So when Ben was a boy, there were plenty of young Franklins in the little wooden house on Milk Street. Ben's mother was busy from morning to night cooking and cleaning and picking up after her big family.

This meant that Ben had to learn how to take care of himself while he was still quite young. He didn't mind. He could always think of something fun to do.

Ben and his friends played tag and hide-and-seek in the busy streets of Boston. They flew kites in nearby farmers' fields. And they climbed trees in the shadowy woods that still pressed so close to town.

But best of all was the water. Boston was an important seaport town. So Ben and his friends spent a lot of time down at the docks, watching the big sailing ships from faraway places. They paddled rafts and canoes on the Charles River. They fished in many different ponds and lakes, and they swam in anything that was more than two feet deep.

Swimming was at the very top of Ben's list of ways to have a good time. He liked it so much that for the rest of his life he would say that things were "going swimmingly" when he meant they were going exactly right.

One day Ben and the others were flying kites near a big pond. The day was warm, and all the running about was making Ben hot. "Let's go swimming!" he shouted.

The other boys thought this was a good idea. So they all tied their kites to anything handy, took off their clothes, and splashed into the water.

Ben paddled around happily for a few minutes. Then he looked across the lake to the far shore, a mile away. It would be fun to swim over there, he thought. Or would it? Ben was a strong swimmer, but a mile was also a long way. Was the swim really worth all that effort?

Then Ben happened to look at his kite, waving around high in the air. And he got an idea. Quickly he climbed out of the water and untied the kite. Holding tight to the cord, he hopped back in the water again.

"What are you doing, Ben?" one of his friends called out.

"It's an experiment," Ben answered. "You'll have to wait and see if it works."

It did. The wind blew the kite, and the kite pulled Ben. It pulled him all the way across the pond, and he didn't have to do a bit of work.

Not long after that Ben had another idea about how to make swimming easier and more fun. He made two oval-shaped wooden paddles for his feet. With them tied on, he could go much faster through the water. Ben didn't know it, but he had invented the very first swim fins.

Not every idea he came up with worked out quite so well. Ben's father, Josiah, was a very religious man. Every morning and every night he led family prayers. He prayed

before each family meal, too. Often those prayers lasted a long time, and Ben thought he would never get to eat.

One day he and his father were working together, packing salted meat into a big barrel. They would eat this meat for weeks to come. Ben thought about the prayers that would be said at every one of those meals. Then a very practical idea popped into his head—and straight out of his mouth.

"Why don't you just say one long prayer over the whole barrel, Father?" Ben asked. "It would certainly save a lot of time." Mr. Franklin was not amused.

Another of Ben's ideas made his father even more unhappy. It started when Ben and his friends decided to go fishing. They knew just where to go. The biggest fish almost always seemed to swim in the shallow waters of a nearby salt marsh. There was only one problem with this marsh. The edges of it were always muddy.

"I'm tired of getting mud in my shoes," Ben complained.

"Me, too," another boy agreed. "But what can we do about it?"

Then Ben noticed some men building a house not far away. They were building it with stones. Ben began to smile. "I have an idea," he said.

Ben's idea was to take some of those stones and build a small wharf with them. "Then we can stand on it and keep our feet dry."

"But won't the workmen mind?" someone asked.

"They won't know anything about it," Ben answered. "We'll wait until they quit for the day. Don't worry, there are plenty of stones for everyone."

So the boys waited until the workmen went home to dinner. Then they carted the stones to the edge of the marsh. Some of the stones were heavy. It took three boys to carry one of them. But they kept on, for they'd caught some of Ben's excitement.

Finally the wharf was done. Ben and the others stood back to admire their work. "Now we can fish in true comfort!" Ben exclaimed. "Let's meet back here tomorrow morning."

But next morning the workmen realized that many of their stones were missing. And

it didn't take them long to find out v
they'd gone or to discover who had built the
wharf.

Ben and his friends were in big trouble.
"What made you do such a thing?" his father shouted.

"But, Father," Ben tried to explain. "It's
so useful. Come and see for yourself how well
it's built."

"No, Benjamin," said his father with a
stern frown. "What is not honest can never
be truly useful. What's more, you and your
friends will return every one of those stones.
Now!"

For the next few hours a sadder but wiser
group of boys hauled the rocks back where
they came from. Every one seemed at least
three times heavier than it had the night before.

Ben loved having a good time. But sometimes he said, "No, not now," when his
friends came by to play. For he also loved to
read. Ben couldn't remember when he
learned to read. He just knew that from the
beginning, books were a kind of magic for

him. They took him so many places and told him so many things.

Books were not very common in the early 1700s. Many families had none at all. Ben's father did have some religious books. But there were no pictures in them. And the words were long and strange. Ben read them anyway. Then he set out to find as many other books as he could.

Sometimes a friend of the family would lend him one. Every once in a while his father gave him a few coins to spend. Ben always saved those coins until he had enough to buy a battered second-hand book. Often the cover was torn and the pages were tattered and stained. But Ben didn't care. For nothing could take away the wonderfulness of those printed words.

Not many children went to school when Ben was growing up—certainly not tradesmen's children like Ben. It cost too much money. But Mr. Franklin saw how bright and eager to learn his youngest son was. So when Ben was eight, he sent him to school.

Before long Ben was at the head of his class in every subject except one. For some reason he just couldn't learn arithmet. This didn't bother him much, though. It was words, words, words that Ben Franklin wanted more of!

Ben loved school, but he didn't stay there long. After two years, when Ben was ten years old, his father had to tell him that his school days were over. Mr. Franklin worked hard as a candle and soap maker. He made enough money to take care of his large family. But that was all. He simply could not afford to pay for Ben's schooling any longer.

Since Ben was not going to school, he had to learn a trade. Mr. Franklin thought about sending Ben to apprentice with another tradesman, but he decided against this. Although Mr. Franklin didn't approve of Ben's sense of humor nor did he always like Ben's big ideas, he was still very fond of his son. So he decided to keep Ben at home and teach him to be a candle and soap maker.

For the next two years Ben learned how to dip candles that were slim and straight. He learned how to make soap that was creamy and smooth. There was only one thing wrong—he hated every last minute of it.

The hot wax splattered. The fat that was used to make soap smelled terrible. Besides, it was boring. And that was what bothered Ben most of all.

Ben began to slip away from the shop more and more. He spent most of this time down on the docks. He watched sailors unloading the big ships from faraway lands. It all looked like grand fun—so much fun that Ben decided he'd found just the job he wanted to do.

When Ben told his parents that he wanted to be a sailor, his mother started to cry. His father tried to talk him out of it. After all, just a few years before, their son Josiah had sailed away on one of those big ships and never been heard from again. It was almost certain that he'd been shipwrecked. One son was enough. Mr. Franklin was determined not to lose Ben, too.

Mr. Franklin tried to reason with him. That didn't work. Finally he simply ordered Ben not to go to sea.

Ben said, "Yes, sir." But his father knew he had to find a trade that Ben liked—and fast—or Ben might run away to sea anyway.

So he began to take Ben on walks around Boston.

Boston was a bustling town, and there were plenty of other tradesmen to watch. Ben saw carpenters and bricklayers and metal workers. He saw people who worked in pewter and brass and silver.

At the end of each walk Mr. Franklin asked Ben if he'd had a good time. And Ben always said yes. He liked to watch skilled people at work. But when his father asked if he would like to be a carpenter or a bricklayer or a metal worker, Ben said no. He still wanted to go to sea.

Poor Mr. Franklin. He was almost at his wit's end. What was he going to do with this stubborn boy of his? Then he had one last idea. What was the one thing Ben loved more than anything? Books!

Suddenly Mr. Franklin knew the place for Ben. Another son of his had just opened a print shop, right in the heart of Boston. Yes, that was the answer. He would send Ben to work for James.

Twelve-year-old Ben didn't know it, but his true education was about to begin.

Ben Learns a Trade

BEN BECAME HIS BROTHER JAMES'S AP-
prentice, and he signed a contract to
work for him until he was twenty-one years
old. Only during the last year would he be
paid.

Ben promised a lot of things when he
signed that paper. He promised to obey
James. He promised to keep his secrets. He
promised not to get married. He promised
not to go to taverns and not to gamble.

In return for all this James made some
promises, too. He promised to feed Ben and
to give him a place to sleep. Finally he promised to teach him to be a printer. Ben had a
feeling right from the start that *he* was making too many promises, and James too few.
But as he said years later, "I always did have
an instinct to make the best of something I
couldn't avoid."

So Ben settled down and began to learn as
much as he could about the printing trade.

Soon he could wash and sort and set type. He learned how to keep the printing press in working order, and how to run off page after page of clean, readable print. Before long he discovered that he actually liked this job.

There was something else that Ben liked about this time in his life—there were so many more books to read. Right next door to the print shop was a friendly bookseller. He often loaned Ben a book. James also had a friend with a good-sized library. Ben could borrow books from him, too. One way or another Ben had plenty to read.

But James was a strict taskmaster. He worked all his apprentices long and hard. He worked Ben hardest of all, for he didn't want anyone to think he was playing favorites, just because Ben was his brother. So Ben had to find reading time in bits and snatches.

He would wake up at dawn and read a few pages before work. He would read by candlelight until the wick guttered out, late at night. On Sunday, his only day off, he also read.

Then one day Ben thought of a way to make more time for his precious books. His

brother James and all the apprentices lived at a nearby boardinghouse. They ate their meals there, too. The main course at most of these meals was meat.

Ben had read a book about the benefits of a vegetarian diet. The book said that meat was heavy and full of "evil humours"—that a diet of vegetables and fruits and nuts would clean up the system and keep the mind sharp.

Ben wasn't at all sure what "evil humours" were, but he did know one thing. Meat was expensive, and vegetables were very cheap. So Ben went to his brother. "Give me half the money you spend feeding me every week, and I will feed myself," he said.

This sounded like a crazy bargain to James. But then his little brother was always coming up with strange ideas, and James liked to save money as much as the next man. So he said yes.

After that, when the others left the print shop for their meals, Ben stayed behind. He fed himself on vegetables—and the rich ideas in books.

Ben was interested in everything: history, science, travel books, fiction, and biographies. Especially interesting to him was any book about how to do something. All his life Ben would like such useful information. He even read a book called *Essays to Do Good* and decided this was very practical, too.

Ben also spent much of his precious free time trying to improve his writing skills.

Soon after Ben began work at the print shop he tried his hand at poetry. His first poem was titled "The Lighthouse Tragedy." It was about a sea captain and his family who drowned in a terrible storm.

The poem was full of people saying things like "Oh, father! Oh, mother! Save me!" and "Alas, I die!" Reading lines like that made his eyes fill up with tears.

Ben's second poem was about a famous pirate named Teach. Sometimes he would speak the opening lines aloud to himself, just to hear how grand they sounded.

> Will you hear of a bloody battle,
> Lately fought upon the seas?
> It will make your ears rattle
> And your admiration cease.

Ben thought this poem was even better than his first. His father didn't quite agree. Mr. Franklin said that Ben's spelling and handwriting were just fine. But his use of words was "horrible." And his style was clumsy and slipshod.

Poor Ben. At first he was very hurt by his father's blunt words, but Ben could never fool himself for long. When he studied the poems again, he began to see that his father was right. They weren't very good. In fact, they were horrible.

What could he do about it? He wasn't in school anymore. He had no teacher to help him develop his writing skills. Well, then, Ben decided, he'd have to do it himself.

But how? Ben soon worked out a way. First he took a book he especially admired and read a chapter or two. He put the book aside for several weeks. Then he remembered what he had read and tried to write it down in his own words. Finally he went back and compared the two pieces of work.

His never measured up to the original, of course. But he knew that the faults could be corrected—once he figured out what they were. Ben did this exercise time and again, and gradually his writing improved.

Then Ben realized that to become a truly good writer, he needed to learn more words, so he figured out a way to do that, too. Once more he read a chapter or two in a book. Then he took those chapters and turned them into verse. Finally he rewrote them in sentence form. This wasn't easy, for the poems had to have words that rhymed. But it worked and he learned many new words.

Ben did something else to improve his writing skills. After reading he made notes on separate pieces of paper. Then he took those notes and jumbled them like a deck of cards. He put them away for a while. Finally he tried to put them together again in the proper order. This, he said, helped him learn how to write and think in an orderly way.

For three years Ben struggled all alone, reading everything he could and trying to become a good writer. He was sure that he was getting better. But just how much was hard to tell.

Then, in the summer of 1721, James decided to start a newspaper. Some of his friends thought this was a silly idea. There were already two newspapers in Boston, and it wasn't a very big city. So how could he expect to succeed?

But James decided to go ahead anyway. And he was right. Soon the *New England Courant* was by far the most popular newspaper in town. And for very good reason. The other two papers were full of dull things like last Sunday's sermons, lists of what ships were sailing that week, notices about runaway cows and pigs, and stale news items from faraway countries such as England.

The *New England Courant* was interested in much more lively and close-to-home subjects. It ran articles criticizing government leaders. Sometimes it also criticized the rich and powerful, who lived in splendid homes on Boston's North Side and often didn't have to work at all. Finally it took on the Puritan ministers, a group of men who often believed that life was serious and full of sin and pain, as well.

The men who wrote for the *New England Courant* were young, often poor, and always full of high spirits. So they had a grand time poking fun at Boston's ruling classes. They were also some of the brightest minds in town. And they knew they could get in real trouble for what they were doing. So they signed their work with fanciful false names—such as Ichabod Henroost, Fanny Mournful, and Harry Meanwell.

Oh, how Ben longed to write for the newspaper, too! He was bursting with ideas to share. But he knew that James would never let him express any of them. After all, he was just a little brother and a lowly apprentice.

What if *he* wrote under a false name, too? That might work. So he invented a character named Silence Dogood and put his own thoughts and opinions in her name.

Ben couldn't just hand these articles to James, of course. So he slipped them under the print shop door late at night.

And James printed them. James thought they were terrific, in fact. And so did his friends. Often they sat around trying to guess who this wonderful writer *really* was. Ben thought he would explode with pride.

In Ben's first article Silence Dogood described herself. "I am courteous and good humored (unless I am first provoked), and handsome, and sometimes witty . . ." Which was, of course, a good description of Ben.

And Silence, like Ben, had a great deal to say about almost everything. She talked about the kind of religious people who took themselves too seriously (she was against that), the sin of pride (she was against that, too), education for women (that she was for), public drunkenness (against), and freedom of thought and speech (for). Silence had *lots* to say about that.

In the person of Silence Dogood young Ben Franklin wrote: "Without freedom of thought there can be no such thing as wisdom . . ."

And "I am a mortal enemy of arbitrary government and unlimited power. I am naturally very jealous for the rights and liberties of my country . . ."

Seventeen-year-old Benjamin Franklin had no idea that fifty years from then—more than half a lifetime away—he would be ready to defend those same words as America prepared to fight for her freedom from England.

Silence Dogood often spoke of freedom of thought and speech. But Ben's freeness of thought and speech didn't please James.

And when James found out Ben was Silence Dogood, *this* didn't please him, either. Ben had a quick tongue. And James had a quick temper. These two traits were not a good mix. The brothers fought more and more about almost everything. And when this happened, James often got so angry that he hit Ben. Ben didn't hit back. But he did get furious and frustrated.

Ben had by now learned as much as he could about printing. He was very good at it. Yet he had almost five more years before his apprenticeship was over. Five long years before he could be free to do as he pleased. No, Ben thought, that was just too long to wait.

As usual Ben soon put his thoughts into action. It was time to strike out on his own. So he did. Seventeen-year-old Benjamin Franklin decided to run away.

Ben Runs Away

BEN NEEDED MONEY TO GET OUT OF TOWN. So he sold the few precious books he'd managed to collect over the years. Then he bought a ticket on a ship that was about to sail south.

Three days later Ben was in New York City. As soon as he stepped off the ship, he started to look for work as a printer's helper. But in 1723 New York was little more than a village. Ben discovered that there was only one printer in the whole town. And he didn't need any help.

The printer did make a suggestion—why didn't Ben try Philadelphia? It was larger than New York. Surely Ben would be able to find a job there.

Ben thought this was a fine idea. But how could he get there? Philadelphia was in the colony of Pennsylvania—more than one hundred miles farther south. And he was almost out of money. He didn't even have enough to buy a ticket on a common coach. No, he'd have to walk most of the way, like other poor people did.

First Ben had to get across New York Harbor to New Jersey. He went down to the waterfront and finally found a rickety little ferryboat that was about to make the trip. He handed over one of his few remaining coins and climbed aboard.

Soon a terrible storm struck. Dark clouds rolled across the sky. Thunder rumbled. Lightning flashed. Ben and the other passengers huddled together as icy rain poured down in sheets. The fierce wind ripped at their ragged sails. Soon it had blown them completely off course, into the outer harbor. For thirty hours Ben and the others were tossed about in that rolling, pitching boat before the storm finally died down and the boat was able to land in New Jersey.

But Ben's troubles were far from over. The wind had died. But the rain continued to pour down heavily. For almost three days Ben walked through it. His only relief was a few hours of damp rest each night in some rough and usually buggy inn. But it was too late to turn back now. Finally, just as the rain was beginning to let up he came to the town of Burlington, on the Delaware River.

From there he needed to find a boat that would take him downriver to Philadelphia. But there was none. Someone told him he'd just missed one and would very likely have to wait for days to get another.

"I was beginning to wish now I had never left home," Ben wrote later. But in the evening, a small sailing boat did drift into sight.

"Are you going to Philadelphia?" Ben called.

The captain of the boat admitted that he was, but at first he said he couldn't take Ben. The boat was too crowded already. He must have been touched by the unhappy look on Ben's face, though. "Oh, all right," he decided, "you're not so big. Hop in."

Later he was glad that he did. As night fell, the breeze died away. They would have to row the rest of the way. Ben, who had been in and out of boats most of his life, was glad to lend a hand.

"We ought to be in Philadelphia by midnight," the captain said. But fate had one more little trick in store. A thick fog sprang up. They couldn't see anything at all.

"We'll have to stop and wait the weather out," the captain decided. "Who can tell? We may already have passed Philadelphia."

The boat pulled in to shore. For the rest of the night Ben sat on the bank with the others around a small fire. He tried to sleep. But the cold, and his glum thoughts, kept him awake. Would he never get to Philadelphia? Maybe the place simply didn't exist!

As soon as day broke, however, one of the passengers exclaimed, "I know where we are! Philadelphia is right around the next bend!" A few minutes later Ben got his first glimpse of the town that he would call home for the rest of his life.

He was tired and dirty. He had no money and no job. He didn't know a single soul in the whole city.

Ben began to smile anyway. For it was a new day. The sun was shining. And he was sure that his luck was about to take a turn for the better. At last.

Ben was right. He soon found a job in a print

shop—a paying job. He found a place to stay with a nice family, the Reads, who had a seventeen-year-old daughter named Debbie. She and Ben quickly became friends. Ben also began to make friends with some young men who worked around town.

A few months after he arrived in Philadelphia, Ben's life took a truly extraordinary turn. It began with a letter he received from a brother-in-law named Robert Holmes.

Ben hadn't told his family in Boston where he was yet. He was afraid they'd try to make him go back. But somehow Robert Holmes had discovered his secret. Now he wrote Ben, telling him how worried the family was. Everyone, except James, had forgiven him for running away, he wrote. Now they just wanted him to come home.

All his life Benjamin Franklin would love to write letters. "They were an important part of my advancement," he said. Now Ben wrote to his brother-in-law. The words flowed from his pen as he explained why he'd been so unhappy in Boston and why he was so happy now in Philadelphia.

Robert Holmes was a sea captain, sailing

up and down the coast of America. When he received Ben's reply, he happened to be staying for a few days with the governor of Pennsylvania, Sir William Keith.

He showed his host Ben's letter. The governor was very impressed. "I am astonished at how well this young man expresses himself!" he exclaimed. "See how convincingly he puts down his arguments. Yes, he has a fine way with words. He should not waste this talent working for someone else."

Just a few days later, to everyone's amazement, Governor Keith strode into the place where Ben was working. After paying him some compliments Sir William said, "Why don't you open up your own print shop? I am sure you would be a big success."

Ben was terribly flattered, of course. But he didn't take the governor seriously at first. "It's good of you to say such kind words, sir," he answered. "But I have no money to buy type or a press, much less rent a shop."

"Nonsense." Sir William waved this problem away. "You have a father, don't you?"

Ben nodded.

"Well, then, it's simple. Go to him and borrow the money. I'm sure he will lend it to such a promising lad."

Ben was not nearly so sure. "I don't think he will, sir. He's . . . he's not very happy with me right now."

"Well, then," said Sir William in a grand tone of voice, "I will write him a letter telling him just how good *I* think you are. Surely *that* will carry the day."

Suddenly Ben felt a spurt of excitement. Maybe, just maybe, this wonderful scheme had some chance of working after all.

Governor Keith wrote the letter and placed it in a big envelope with his special government seal. A few days later Ben, with the letter in his pocket and his head full of dreams, left for Boston.

It was a very different Ben. He was dressed in a fine suit. He had a pocket full of silver coins. He even owned a watch, a rare thing in Ben's day.

His father was not impressed with the new Ben or with the governor's letter.

"What manner of man would think of setting up a mere boy in his own business?" he demanded. "Why, you won't be twenty-one for three years yet!"

"But, sir, he's governor of Pennsylvania."

"I don't care who he is," Mr. Franklin snapped. "He's still lacking in common sense."

And that was that. A very downcast Ben Franklin returned to Philadelphia.

Then Sir William had another idea. "I see your father is not a daring thinker," he said. "But I am. *I* will lend you the money myself."

He told Ben to get ready to set sail for England. That was the best place to buy all the equipment he would need to set up a shop. "I will give you a letter of credit," Sir William continued. "With that in hand you will have no trouble getting some of the money I have in a London bank."

But whenever Ben came by for this particular letter, Sir William always seemed too busy to write it, and he asked Ben to return the following day.

The day before the ship was to sail Ben went once more. Again the governor

32

couldn't see him. Too busy. He sent a servant with a message, though. The letter of credit would be sent to the ship in a sealed bag with some other letters Sir William was sending to England. Ben could collect it when the ship docked.

Ben arrived in London on Christmas Eve 1724 and discovered he had been tricked. There was no letter of credit. There was nothing at all for him in that sack. Later he learned that Governor Keith had deceived others, too. The governor had no money, but he liked to please people. So he simply gave empty promises instead.

Poor Ben. Here he was again, alone and without money in a strange town—and in a strange country. The huge Atlantic Ocean separated him from everything and everyone he knew.

For a few minutes he was gripped by panic. Then he started to think. He had a strong body and a good mind. London was one of the literary centers of the world. Surely there were many print shops here, shops that would be happy to hire a skilled printer. Besides—Ben's eyes began to sparkle just a little—from what he'd seen so far, London seemed like a wonderfully exciting place to explore.

Once more Ben bounced back. He found a job and a place to stay. Before long he started making friends. Ben went with his friends to see his first play in London. He saw his first concert there, too. And he had many good and memorable conversations. For London was filled with people who had intelligent and witty things to say.

Ben had a terrific time. Only one thing continued to bother him. He was home-sick. So after staying in London for eighteen months, Ben sailed back to America.

On that journey home Ben did some serious thinking. So far he'd had a grand life. He'd traveled, made new friends and had lots of adventures. But he hadn't *accomplished* very much. If he should die now, what could anyone say of him? That he was a good fellow? That he knew how to have fun? No, Ben decided, he wanted more from life than that. It was time to settle down.

Ben Settles Down

ONCE BEN DECIDED THIS, HE DREW UP A plan of how to behave. He vowed to live simply and never waste money. He would be honest in both word and deed. He promised himself never to speak badly of anyone, even if it was true. And finally he was determined to work hard at whatever he was doing, "for industry and patience are the surest means of arriving at plenty."

Ben Franklin said he followed this plan—on the whole—"quite through old age."

The next few years were busy ones for him. As soon as he got back to Philadelphia, he found a job in another printing house. He saved most of his salary. Then he borrowed some more and made his old dream come true. He opened his own print shop.

And that wasn't all. In 1730 Ben married. His wife's name was Debbie. She was the daughter of the family he'd stayed with when he first came to Philadelphia. Ben was happy being married. "A single man," he liked to say, "is like the odd half of a pair of scissors." Then Debbie and Ben became the parents of a boy named William. This made him happier still.

About this same time Ben started a newspaper. He called it the *Pennsylvania Gazette*. He wrote many of the articles himself and the *Gazette* was soon a big success.

Then Ben started still another business—a kind of general store right next door to his print shop. This was Debbie's special pride and joy. She spent many hours a day waiting on customers who wanted Bibles and dictionaries, paper and pencils, wine and cheese and codfish cakes, soap and sealing wax. The busy young Franklins even sold what they called fresh goose feathers, from a live goose they kept in the backyard.

The year 1732 was Ben's busiest yet. His second son, Francis, was born. His printing press and newspaper were both doing well. So was his general store. Now he thought up something new to do. He started to publish an almanac. And it soon proved to be his biggest success of all.

Books were scarce in Ben's day. Many households had only two—the Bible and the almanac, for that year. These were the books most people felt they could not live without.

An almanac showed the days and weeks and months of the year, and when the moon would be full. It told the time of sunrise and sunset on different days, and when high and low tide would be. It forecast the weather for the year to come. It also contained recipes, riddles, jokes, songs, and odd facts of all sorts. All in all, it was a very handy book.

Years before, Ben had used Silence Dogood to express his thoughts and opinions. Now, for his almanac, he invented another make-believe person to serve the same purpose. This character was a poor man named Richard Saunders. So Ben called his almanac *Poor Richard's Almanac.*

Poor Richard was make-believe, but Ben drew him so well that a great many people believed he was a real person. Often they would say, "I wonder what Poor Richard has to say about this. Let's go look in the almanac and find out."

Ben's almanac was popular because it was

different from all the others being published at the time. In addition to its practical information, it also contained all sorts of sayings and quotations. Some of these Ben made up himself. Some he took from other books. When he did, he carefully rewrote them until each one was sharp and easily understood. And he ended them all with "says Poor Richard."

Poor Richard had opinions about almost everything. Some of his sayings were funny. For example, Poor Richard said, "Three may keep a secret, if two of them are dead." And "He that lies down with dogs shall rise up with fleas." And "Fish and visitors stink after three days."

Some of the sayings of Poor Richard were wise. He said, "A mob's a monster—heads enough but no brains." "Being poor is no shame, but being ashamed of it is." And "God helps those that help themselves."

Some of his sayings were both funny and wise. It was Poor Richard's opinion that "If your head is wax, don't walk in the sun." "Keep your eyes wide open before marriage, half shut afterwards." And "A man between

two lawyers is like a fish between two cats."

Ben was very concerned about money—how best to make it and how best not to lose it. Poor Richard said things like "Beware of little expenses. A small leak will sink a great ship." "A penny saved is a penny earned." And "Honesty is the best policy."

But it was the subject of time that was at the heart of Benjamin Franklin's personal philosophy. Naturally Poor Richard had lots to say concerning this: "Up sluggard, and waste not life. In the grave will be sleeping enough." "Lost time is never found again." And "Early to bed, early to rise, makes a man healthy, wealthy, and wise."

Ben's first almanac sold mostly in the Philadelphia area, but by the time the second was published, people all over Pennsylvania were buying the book. Only a few years later it had become the most popular book in the American colonies, and many of Poor Richard's sayings were being translated into foreign languages as well.

People everywhere had taken Ben's almanac to their hearts because it was so much like him—helpful, practical, and a lot of fun.

41

Ben Branches Out

BEN ADORED HIS SONS, AND IT WAS A COM-
mon sight to see big Ben, William, and
little Francis walking hand-in-hand through
the streets of Philadelphia.

Ben and his wife were fond of each other,
but they had very little in common. Debbie
was a simple woman. She could barely read
or write. She was interested in very little except her family and the shop she ran so well.

Ben, of course, was interested in everything, and he always found time for his
friends. He simply could not live happily
without what he called their "sweet society."

Ben liked to quote a famous philosopher
who said he'd rather be the stupidest block-
head in the world than be someone who
knew everything—but had no one intelligent to communicate it to. One way Ben had
solved this need was to start a club called the
Junto. At every meeting Ben and his friends
discussed something that interested them.

Sometimes these discussions were very serious. One evening they raised the question "Have you read anything recently that is remarkable or suitable to be communicated to the Junto, particularly in history, morality, poetry, physics, travel, or mechanical arts?"

Ben and his friends in the Junto weren't always serious. During the warm months of the year they often took long walks in the country, stopping at some pleasant place to picnic. Sometimes they just sat around laughing and joking and making up songs.

Ben and the other members also wanted to help improve the daily life of others. One of the questions they discussed often was "Can you think of anything in which the Junto may be of service to mankind, to their country, and to their friends?" As usual Ben had a great many ideas.

For as long as he could remember, books had been an absolute necessity for him. Now Ben thought of a way to make books available to others. He suggested that all the members of the Junto gather their books together in one place. Then each of them would have many more books to read.

Soon Ben began to think of all the other people in Philadelphia. Why shouldn't they be able to read, too? So he suggested that these books be available to all the citizens of the city. Anyone could borrow the books for a small sum each year. This money would go toward buying still more books, and so the list would grow.

It was 1731 when Ben Franklin started the first public library in America. From the beginning it was a great success. As he put it, "Reading became quite fashionable."

In Ben's day there were no fire engines or fire fighters in Philadelphia to put out a blaze. If a building caught fire, it just burned down, and often burned everything else around it. In 1735 Ben began writing articles about this in his newspaper. He discussed ways of preventing fires and he said, "An ounce of prevention is worth a pound of cure."

"Be careful not to carry red-hot coals from one place to another, unless they are covered in some way," he advised. And "Be sure to keep your chimneys swept clean, for dirty chimneys burn most furiously."

Ben knew, however, it would take more than prevention to stop the fires that so often raged through entire neighborhoods. It would also take direct and immediate action. So in December 1736 he organized the first volunteer fire brigade in Philadelphia. It was called the Union Fire Company.

Soon other companies were formed. Before long they made a kind of network all over town. Philadelphia became safer from fire than any other city in the colonies.

Next Ben turned his attention to something else that plagued the daily life of every Philadelphian. This was dirt. There was not a single paved street in the city. People had to walk through clouds of dust in dry weather and wade through mud in wet. So Ben campaigned until a bill was passed to pave the streets.

He also noticed that when carriages passed his house, they often left a dirty trail on the new pavement that he and his family couldn't help but track inside. Ben talked to his neighbors about this and got them all to give a little money to hire a man to sweep the dirt into piles twice a week. Horse-drawn carts hauled away the dirt and other rubbish. From this small beginning the whole idea of sanitation departments and garbage collection would grow.

It was Ben who suggested plans that led to a more efficient police force. He worked out a way to improve the lighting of streets. He published a paper on the benefits of higher education which led to the establishment of the Philadelphia Academy. This school would later become the University of Pennsylvania. He also helped to form the first hospital in America.

No wonder more and more people said, "Go to Franklin if you want to get something done."

Only one thing saddened Ben during these busy and successful years. In 1736 Ben's son Francis, at the age of four, died of smallpox. Ben would mourn his son for the rest of his long life. As he wrote thirty-six years later, "I have seldom since seen him equaled in everything, and to this day I cannot think of him without a sigh."

Ben Flies a Kite

"**W**ORK HARD AND SAVE AS MUCH AS you can for that is the way to wealth." This good advice from Poor Richard worked for Ben. By the late 1740s he felt he had made enough money to do something he'd wanted to do for a long time—stop being a businessman.

Forty-two-year-old Ben retired "to read, write letters, to think, study, and talk with worthy men on points that may produce something for the common benefit of mankind . . ." Even though he was retired, he was busier than ever. Ben studied foreign languages. He wanted to learn as many as he could so that he would be able to read books written by authors from other countries. Before he was done, he had taught himself French, Italian, Spanish, and Latin.

Ben had always had an overwhelming curiosity about how things worked. And many scientific discoveries he was to make in the future were based on simple observation. He had, as a friend noted, a way of looking under the surface of things.

One day Ben was taking a walk in the country when he noticed a particular field. A few parts of it were much greener than the rest. Someone else might have wondered at the sight for a minute or two, and then walked on. Not Ben. He searched out the owner of the field and discovered that gypsum, a white powdery mineral, had been accidentally dropped on those lush spots.

What could this mean? "I say that gypsum should be spread on any field under cultivation," he announced. "For I believe it will make crops grow better." At the time, nobody paid any attention to this observation. But Ben had been the first person ever to suggest using artificial fertilizer.

In the course of his long life Ben took a number of trips back and forth across the Atlantic Ocean. During those trips he found something fascinating to study even in the middle of all those endless miles of blue seas.

What he noticed was a wide band of water that was different from the rest of the ocean around it. He called it a river that ran through the sea. He noted that it was a different color. More weeds grew in it. It didn't sparkle at night like the rest of the ocean. Whales didn't seem to swim in it. And it was warmer, too. Ben discovered this by hanging a thermometer over the side of the ship and measuring the water temperature again and again.

So, long before any other scientist, Ben Franklin had discovered and started to chart the Gulf Stream, that great river-in-the-ocean which warms the eastern part of America and much of Europe as well.

Ben was also interested in physical health. He noticed that some workers, such as printers and plumbers and house painters, often came down with the same mysterious wasting disease. Ben investigated the materials these men handled every day. And he discovered that they all worked with the metal lead.

Although Ben was no doctor, he realized that lead must be what was making the workers so sick. And Ben was right. He was the first person ever to diagnose the industrial illness called lead poisoning.

Ben was usually bursting with health. But he did catch a lot of colds, and he was interested in what caused them. Most people thought that fresh air was to blame, especially fresh air breathed at night. They were careful to keep their windows shut tight, no matter how hot and stuffy it got. They also believed that getting wet was dangerous.

Ben didn't agree with any of these ideas. He studied his own life and wrote, "Traveling in severe winters, I have suffered cold sometimes to only short of freezing, but this did not make me catch cold." As for getting wet, he added, it was one of his favorite sports to swim for hours at a time, and that had never given him a cold, either.

No, Ben decided, people caught colds by other means. "I have long been satisfied from observation that people catch colds from one another when shut up together in close rooms," he wrote. This caused them, he added, to breathe in each other's faces.

He also felt that colds were easily caught when a person's home and bed and clothes were dirty. The way to avoid colds, he concluded, was to live cleanly, to eat and drink sensibly, to exercise, and to breathe as much fresh air as possible.

Ben Franklin had never heard of a germ or a virus. Nobody had then. Yet he'd discovered almost all anyone would ever know about the common cold—just by watching and thinking.

Ben wanted to "multiply the conveniences and pleasures of life." So a number of his ideas developed into inventions. Some of these were small, everyday affairs. Some were big enough to change the lives of many people. But they all had one thing in common. Like Ben, they were highly practical.

During the warm months Ben was often bothered by flies buzzing around his head. So he invented a rocking chair with a fan connected to it by a string. When Ben rocked, the fan turned and kept the flies from landing on his balding head.

Often he wanted to get a book from a high shelf. So he invented a long pole with a kind of artificial hand on the end of it. When he pulled a wire the hand closed around his book. Other people were soon copying this contraption of Ben's. Grocers, for example, used it to pull down wares they had stored on their high shelves.

In Ben's day people had only open fireplaces to heat their homes. Ben thought these fireplaces were very poorly designed, because most of the heat went straight up the chimney. The fireplaces also sucked in cold air from outside, through cracks around a room's windows and doors.

"It rushes in at every crevice, so strongly as to make a continual whistling or howling, and 'tis very uncomfortable as well as dangerous to sit against any such crevice," Ben commented. People had to stand very close to a fireplace to get warm at all, and even then they were most often "scorched before and froze behind," as Ben put it.

In 1742 he decided to invent a stove that would solve all these problems. Ben's stove was a big metal box. It heated the whole room, not just a small part of it. As he said, "My common room is made twice as warm as it used to be, with a quarter of the wood I formerly consumed there." People who had this stove saved money, too.

Ben's name for this new way to heat homes was the Pennsylvania Fireplace. But most people called it the Franklin Stove. From the first it was a best-seller. Before long it could be found in homes throughout every American colony. Soon it spread to Europe as well. Ben's humble metal box even found its way into the palaces of kings.

He could have made a fortune on it if he had taken out a patent. Then, anyone who made or sold the Franklin Stove would have had to pay him. But Ben said no to this. "As we enjoy great advantage from the inventions of others, we should be glad of an opportunity to serve others by any invention of ours, and this we should do freely and generously."

Anything scientific fascinated Ben, especially electricity. It was a great mystery in Ben's day. Nobody knew much about it—and the few things people thought they knew were usually wrong. Many people thought electricity was a magical weapon of the gods or something men could only make in special workshops. Ben believed it was simply a fundamental force of nature.

In the late 1740s Ben began to study this infant science. Soon he was so caught up in it that he could hardly think or talk of anything else. "I never was before engaged in any study that so totally engrossed my attention and my time as this has lately done," he wrote to a scientist friend in England.

Benjamin Franklin, as another scientist said later, had a truly fundamental mind. He could grasp a subject as deeply as it was understood at the time, and then go still deeper into it to make fresh discoveries.

In the next several years Ben worked out two of the basic principles of electricity. One—which one day would be known as the electron theory—was the basis for almost all other advances in electricity. Ben's second discovery was of the positive and negative nature of currents.

With such everyday materials as window glass, a few silk cords, lead wire, and some thin lead plates, Ben made the very first electric battery. He thought of it as little more than a toy. There was no way he could know how important it would be one day.

Ben made another vital contribution to this fast-growing science. He created new vocabulary words. Because he and his fellow scientists were breaking such new ground, there were often no specific words to describe what they were dealing with. So, being Ben, he invented them. It was Benjamin Franklin who first used such electrical terms as *armature, battery, charged, condenser, conductor, electrician, brush, plus* and *minus,* and *positive* and *negative.*

Ben had a strong suspicion that electricity and lightning were the same thing. A few others suspected this, too, but it was Ben who designed an experiment to prove that his theory was right.

To do this he had to draw lightning down from a cloud. He already knew that electricity was attracted to sharply pointed objects. So in June of 1752 he fixed a long, pointed metal rod to the top of an ordinary child's kite. To the bottom of the kite string he tied a big iron key. Then he was ready. As he said, "Let the experiment be made!"

All he needed was a good-sized storm. A few days later clouds began to gather. Ben

and his twenty-two-year-old son, William, were standing by the edge of a large field when the rain started. Thunder rumbled overhead and lightning began to flash.

"Go ahead, son," Ben said quietly.

William began to run, with Ben running beside him. Soon the kite was sailing high in the sky. It disappeared into one stormy cloud, and then another. But nothing happened. Ben began to get tired and discouraged. It looked as if this experiment was going to be a failure.

But then Ben noticed something. He saw that the tiny fibers on the string William was holding were standing straight out in the air—as if they were all receiving an electric charge. Ben reached out until his hand was almost touching the metal key. Suddenly a bright blue electric spark jumped from it to his knuckle! He knew it was electricity because he felt the shock. It even made the same crackling sound.

Benjamin Franklin had plucked lightning from the sky! It was the most world-famous experiment of his whole long life. And he'd done it with a simple children's toy.

Ben Goes to England

SUDDENLY BEN WAS FAMOUS. PRAISE AND awards poured in. Everyone wanted to honor the man who had, as one person put it, "stolen fire from heaven."

All this attention pleased Ben, of course. But it didn't make him overly proud. For one thing, he wasn't satisfied with his electrical observations and experiments. So far, he felt, they were just a kind of parlor trick. No, he wouldn't be happy until he found ways to make them truly useful to everyone.

Ben also realized by now how foolish he'd been when he flew his kite on that stormy day. The kite had built up a small charge of electricity—enough to give him a shock. But the kite hadn't been hit by a real bolt of lightning. If it had, Ben most likely would have been killed.

But the whole experience now gave Ben an idea. Every year many houses were struck by lightning and burned to the ground. Ben wondered if that couldn't be prevented. What if people attached a pointed metal rod to the top of their homes? What if they ran a long wire from the rod down the side of the building and into the ground? Then the lightning would be able to follow a path to the earth, *without* burning down the house.

Ben wrote about his idea in the 1753 issue of *Poor Richard's Almanac.* Some people argued against it. They said that lightning was God's weapon for punishing sinners. So it was wrong to outwit God with something man-made like a lightning rod. Somehow this argument never caught on. But Ben's idea did. Soon lightning rods appeared on buildings all over the colonies, and then in foreign lands as well. Once more Ben refused to take out a patent on his idea. Once more he simply gave it to the world.

Now Benjamin Franklin was even more famous. He had not only plucked lightning from the sky, he had tamed it as well. Sadly, though, Ben's days of being a scientist were almost over, for he was continually asked to give his time to public service.

In 1751 he was elected to the Pennsylvania Assembly, the local governing body for the colony.

Then in 1753 he was appointed deputy postmaster general for the northern colonies. The colonial postal service, as Ben soon discovered, didn't work very well. A letter often took months getting from one city to another. Many times it simply never arrived.

Ben decided that before he could straighten out this mess he had to find out, what was causing it. So he spent the next few months traveling by horse from one colony to another. He visited many post offices along the way and listened to local postmasters speak of their problems. Then he helped them work out better solutions. He also figured out ways to improve delivery between the post offices.

Ben loved all this traveling because he saw so many new and exciting things. But in Ben's day travel could also be rough and tiring. Once he had to ride all day through a cold drizzle. After many hours he finally came to an inn. All he could think of was getting close to its fire.

Others had already had the same thought.

61

There was no room left anywhere near the fireplace. So Ben, as usual, had an idea.

"You, there," he called to a servant. "Get a basket of oysters and give it to my horse. Make sure it's a big basket. He's hungry."

The servant looked puzzled. The other people in the tavern were puzzled, too. A horse that ate oysters? They had to see *this* for themselves. They all crowded out of the room. When they came back, they found Ben sitting in a very comfortable chair right by the fire. "Your horse wouldn't touch those oysters," the servant told Ben.

"In that case," he answered, his eyes twinkling, "give the horse some hay and bring the oysters to me!"

All Ben's traveling really paid off. Before he became postmaster general, it often took months for a person in Philadelphia to write someone in Boston and get a letter in return. Ben cut that time to three weeks.

He enjoyed those trips. But he soon noticed that each of the colonies he visited was being run as if it were a separate country. People in one colony had almost nothing to do with those in another. Ben felt this was wrong. The colonists shared many of the same traditions and interests. Why shouldn't they work more closely together?

Ben felt so strongly about this that he drew up a plan. He called it "A Plan for a Union of English Colonies in America." In this document he suggested that the colonies cooperate with one another on such things as trade and defense. Each should send representatives to a common "great council" which would be presided over by a president appointed by the king of England.

The colonists turned the plan down because they felt a president appointed by the king would have too much power. King George II turned it down because he said the plan gave the *colonists* too much power.

Thirty-five years later a form of this American union would come into being. So, as the French writer Honoré de Balzac put it, in addition to all his other inventions, Benjamin Franklin had actually invented the United States of America.

Before the United States came to be, Ben's help was required.

In the 1750s tension was building between

England and her colonies. Ben and most other Americans still thought of themselves as loyal Englishmen. But they also thought they weren't being treated fairly.

Much of the trouble had to do with taxes. In Pennsylvania there had been a running fight between the colonial Assembly and the Penn family for years. Originally the king of England had given this family all the land that was now the colony of Pennsylvania. They still owned huge tracts of land and refused to pay taxes on even one acre of it.

Most Pennsylvanians thought this was terribly unfair. After all, even the king of England paid taxes on land he owned. Finally the Assembly decided to send someone to England to take this matter up with the king. And the person they chose to plead their case was Benjamin Franklin.

Ben thought this job would only take a few months, and then he'd be back home again. He had no way of knowing that he would be in England for much of the next eighteen years.

Ben wanted his wife to go to England with him. But Debbie was desperately afraid of crossing the ocean. The trip often took months, and many ships were lost at sea.

Besides, she knew that Ben would make many grand friends in England. He would move in circles—social and intellectual—where she would be very uncomfortable. So Debbie refused. She would miss her husband very much, but she would stay home.

A daughter had been born to Ben and Debbie in 1743. Ben wanted to take thirteen-year-old Sarah, whom they called Sally, with him. But Debbie said that Sally had to stay and keep her company instead. So in March of 1757 Ben sailed for England with only one member of the family at his side, his son, William.

Ben worked hard for better cooperation between England and her American colonies. But from the first it was an uphill battle. Too many Englishmen looked down on the colonists. "They treat us more like a conquered people than as equals," Ben said.

Then, in 1765, England passed a law that made the colonists explode. This was the Stamp Act. Colonists were required to buy stamps to put on all sorts of things like newspapers and magazines, legal documents, and marriage licenses—even almanacs.

The colonists said this tax was unfair because they had nobody to represent them in the English parliament, the lawmaking body of England.

The colonists fought this unjust law in every way they could. They wrote fiery booklets about it. They refused to buy any goods they had to buy stamps for. And they gathered together in protest meetings that sometimes turned into angry riots.

Benjamin Franklin fought hard while in England to get this hated Stamp Act repealed. Thanks largely to his eloquent arguments, it finally happened. But there were other taxes that led to other angry protests. So year by year the gulf between England and America grew deeper.

In the late 1760s two regiments of British soldiers landed in Boston. They had been sent there to keep the peace. But in March 1770 a fierce street battle broke out. Within minutes five Americans were killed. No one in the colonies would soon forget what they called the Boston Massacre.

"Troops that are sent to the colonies will not find a revolution," Ben said sadly, "but they may well create one."

Ben's job was not a popular one. Because he fought so hard for America's rights, he made many enemies in the English government. But this was still a happy time in his life, for he had not lost his talent for friendship.

Some of Ben's friends were rich and famous. But just as many were poor and unknown. Age was no barrier to friendship, either. Ben was almost seventy now. In physical terms he could be called an old man. But some of Benjamin Franklin's closest friends were children, for he respected them as much as he did anyone else.

One of his young friends was a thirteen-year-old girl named Georgiana Shipley. Ben gave her a most unusual gift: an American gray squirrel which his wife, Debbie, had shipped from Philadelphia.

Mungo, as Georgiana called him, was soon a favorite family pet. But not for long. Somehow Mungo, or Skugg, as they also

sometimes called him, escaped from his cage one day. He was killed by the one family member who did not share this fondness for squirrels—the dog.

A tearful Georgiana buried Mungo in the garden. Then she wrote to Ben and asked him to write something "really fine" to go on the squirrel's tombstone.

Ben was an extremely busy man. But he sat down and wrote, "I lament with you most sincerely the unfortunate end of poor Mungo. Few squirrels were better accomplished, for he has had a good education, traveled far, and seen much of the world . . ." And he ended with the words that were to be placed over the grave:

> Here Skugg
> Lies snug
> As a bug
> In a rug

Ben had many friends in England. But his enemies there were growing in number. They didn't understand what the Americans wanted. Because Ben was the colonists' representative, and because he was there in

London under their noses, these Englishmen held him responsible for everything.

Some government officials even began to call him names such as "snake" and "old doubleface" and "master of mischief." These names didn't hurt Ben. He was much too tough for that. But he realized that it was time to leave England.

On Ben's last day in England he sat trying to read some papers. But often tears filled his eyes and ran down his cheeks. Benjamin Franklin was sad for two reasons. His wife Debbie had died just a few months before, and he knew that he had failed to keep the peace between the two lands he loved most.

He was sure of it now—a terrible war would break out soon.

Ben Goes to France

EN WAS RIGHT. HE WAS STILL SAILING FOR home when the first shots of the Revolutionary War were fired in Lexington, Massachusetts, on April 19, 1775.

Benjamin Franklin had worked long and hard to prevent this war. But it had come anyway, so now he would work even harder to help America win it.

Soon after he returned, he was appointed to the Second Continental Congress, which was in charge of helping the colonies work together to win the war. In the next few months he served on many of its committees. Then, in the spring of 1776, he was picked to be on the most important one of all—the committee to draw up the Declaration of Independence.

This was a document that explained to the world why America felt it could no longer be ruled by England. Ben didn't write it. Thomas Jefferson did. Some people said that Jefferson had been picked because his writing style was so grave and lofty. But others said that Ben had *not* been chosen to write it because the Founding Fathers feared he might slip in some of his funny sayings.

On July 4, 1776, Ben and the other members of the Continental Congress gathered to vote on this important statement. It was truly a sad moment for Ben. He loved both America and England. For many years he had fought to keep them a part of the same family of nations. Now they were engaging in a bitter and bloody struggle.

Ben had a more personal reason for being sad. His own family had been torn apart, too. Ben had always been especially close to his son, William. But William would not be at his side in the coming conflict. William Franklin had decided he must remain loyal to England. Never again would father and son be true friends. But Ben didn't let anyone know what he was thinking. That wasn't his way.

John Hancock was the first man to sign the Declaration of Independence. Before he did, he looked around at the others and said in a very solemn voice, "Let there be no mistake. We must be unanimous about this. There must be no pulling in different ways. We must all hang together."

"Yes," Ben answered, with a twinkle in his eyes. "We must *indeed* all hang together. Or most assuredly we shall all hang separately."

Everyone there thought Ben's remark was funny. But they knew it was deadly serious, too. They must win this war, or they would lose their homes, their lands, and very likely their lives—for England would be sure to execute many of these leaders as traitors.

But *could* they win? Weapons, food, clothing, soldiers, everything needed to keep an army going, was in short supply. It was plain to everyone that the colonies had to have outside assistance to win the revolution. The Founding Fathers decided to ask Benjamin Franklin to go to France to seek help.

Ben wasn't at all sure they'd made the right choice. He was no longer young. He was worn out from hard work, and he wasn't in good health. Often he suffered from gout, a painful swelling of the legs and feet.

But as usual when he was asked to serve,

he didn't refuse. "I fear there is little left of me to be useful," he commented, "but if you want this servant, he will go." There was no way for Ben Franklin to know just how successful his years in France were going to be.

Ben was always happiest when he was surrounded by young people. So, in October of 1776, he and two of his grandsons, Temple and Benny, climbed aboard the sloop *Reprisal* and set sail for France.

This was Ben's fourth trip across the Atlantic Ocean. And it was by far his most difficult. In addition to the always painful gout, he broke out in boils. His head was covered with an itchy rash. And his teeth ached so much that he could only eat the softest foods. Later Benjamin Franklin wrote that the trip "almost demolished me."

By the time he finally landed in France he was so weak that he could only stand by leaning heavily on a stout stick. No wonder he was depressed.

Ben, however, didn't stay gloomy for long. A few minutes later a rickety old carriage came into view, pulled by an equally old, swaybacked horse. Ben took one look and

74

started to laugh. "It *looks* the way I *feel*," he said. "So we're a perfect match!"

Ben and the two boys climbed in and drove off alone on the last leg of their journey. But they weren't alone for long. The French people heard that Benjamin Franklin of America had landed. By the next morning ordinary people—shopkeepers and farmers and housewives—began to leave their work and gather by the side of the road to catch a glimpse of him.

Many called out cheery greetings. "*Bonjour*, Dr. Franklin! We are glad that are you here!"

Ben was astonished. It was hard for him to believe that they knew him at all. But they did. Benjamin Franklin was the man who had brought electricity down from the sky with a simple kite. He was the man who had protected their homes with his lightning rod. And it was he who had written all those funny and wise sayings year after year in *Poor Richard's Almanac*. Many of them now called him "Friend Richard."

Ben was pleased with all this loving attention, of course. But at the same time he was a

little embarrassed, for he was definitely not feeling nor looking his best. Usually Ben dressed carefully in the latest style of the day. In France that meant fancy silk or satin suits with layers of fine lace at the cuffs, and tall white powdered wigs.

Ben, though, was still in the clothes he'd worn on the ship. His coat was made of plain brown cloth. In his hand was a cane instead of a sword. And on his head was an old fur cap. Being several sizes too big, it often slipped down over his eyes. The cap kept his ears warm, and it hid the rash that still covered his head.

Before long, though, Ben began to realize something quite remarkable. The people didn't mind his unfashionable look. As a matter of fact, they liked it. His plain appearance went with their picture of America—a land of simple and natural and honest people.

Ben knew that being liked was a very important part of his job. If the common people approved of him, it would be easier for them to approve of his country, as well. Since Ben liked to invent different characters, he decided to play one now. If simple clothes and unpowdered hair made him a hero, then he'd continue to dress simply. So for the rest of his years in France, Benjamin Franklin stood out in any group because of all the fancy clothes he *didn't* wear.

As the days passed, the French people's welcome grew. By the time Ben reached Paris, huge crowds lined his route, cheering and waving small flags and throwing flowers into his carriage. There was no doubt about it, the people of France had taken plain Benjamin Franklin of America to their hearts.

All this love worked a kind of medical miracle on him. When he had first landed, he'd been so ill and weak he could hardly stand. Now he felt full of energy and ready to work, ready to convince the French that they must support the American cause.

Ben Franklin talked to the leaders of the French government about how powerful and dangerous England would be if the colonists were defeated. To French businessmen he talked about all the trade they would one day have with an independent and growing

America. To the common people, his special friends, he talked about liberty and democracy.

From the beginning Ben found that the French government was sympathetic. It allowed some supplies to be shipped secretly to America's struggling army. This helped. But it was not enough. Ben wanted France to sign a treaty with America, a written agreement to send soldiers, supplies, ships, and money to help fight the Revolutionary War.

At first the French refused to sign the treaty because they simply could not see how a poor nation like America could beat a powerful one like England. And the practical French did not like to back a losing side.

Ben set to work convincing them that America had the one thing it needed most— determination and a fierce will to win. Once he kept at this job almost around the clock for eight straight days.

Finally all this effort paid off. In February of 1778, the king of France signed the treaty with the United States. From then on France openly supported America.

Many people said that without Benjamin

Franklin, this treaty would not have been signed. Some also believed that without the treaty the United States of America would never have been born.

Getting the treaty signed was not the only thing Ben did in France. He also wrote speeches and letters, poems and articles, which were printed on a small printing press he set up in his home. He played the harp, the guitar, and other musical instruments. He also enjoyed making up funny songs to sing with his friends.

Ben was almost eighty years old now. But he still swam in the River Seine as often as he could. He played chess at any time of the day or night. He also continued to have a deep interest in science. In August 1783, when the world's first balloon rose in the air near Paris, Ben was there to cheer as loudly as the smallest child in the crowd.

Not everyone was so excited by this strange invention. "It is an amusing sight, true," someone said. "But what *good* is it?"

"What good is a newborn baby?" Ben

shot back. "You will just have to wait until it grows up!"

Ben found other people's inventions just as fascinating as his own. He also kept inventing things himself. Now that he was old, he used two pairs of eyeglasses. One was for close work such as reading. The other was for seeing at a distance. He hated carrying around two pairs of glasses, putting them on and taking them off all the time.

Then he came up with an idea. He took the two pairs of glasses to a glass cutter and had the lenses cut in two. He put half of one lens in the bottom part of the frame and the other half in the top part. This allowed Ben to look down and see things close to him. When he looked up he could see things far away. Ben called these new lenses doubleglasses. But the rest of the world soon named them bifocals.

Ben packed many things into his busy life. As usual, he always found plenty of time for his friends. Many of them were women. In his day many people thought that women weren't as interesting or as intelligent as

81

men. This was a mistake that Benjamin Franklin never made. He loved to talk with women about serious subjects. He loved to flirt with them, too.

Ben even found time to fall in love with a rich widow named Madame Helvétius. Madame Helvétius loved Ben in return. But when he asked her to marry him, she sadly refused for she realized that Ben would one day want to return to America. At age sixty she felt she was too old to start a new life in such a strange land.

Ben kept her as a very special friend, though, and continued to write to her until the end of his life. In one of those letters he said, "It seems to me that things are badly arranged in this world, when I see that two beings so made to be happy together are obliged to separate."

In 1781 the Revolutionary War came to an end. But Benjamin Franklin stayed in France and worked for the United States for almost four more years. During those years he helped write the treaty of peace between the United States and England.

After he signed it, he said to a friend, "May we never have another war! For in my opinion there never was a good war or a bad peace."

Finally Ben was told he could go home. And he was ready. He wrote his sister Jane that he had "done enough for the public." Now it was time "to sit down and spend my evening hours with old friends."

Thomas Jefferson was sent to be the next ambassador. Soon after he arrived, someone asked him, "Have you come to take Franklin's place?"

Thomas Jefferson smiled and shook his head. "I have come to succeed him," he answered. "No one can take his place."

Ben's Last Days

IN 1785 BEN RETURNED TO PHILADELPHIA, the town he'd first seen so long ago. Then he'd been a poor seventeen-year-old runaway with only pennies in his pocket. Now he was Dr. Benjamin Franklin, master of a number of different professions. Then he'd been a stranger. Now bells rang, cannons boomed, and crowds of eager well-wishers lined the streets to welcome him home.

There were speeches and ceremonies and celebrations all week to honor the return of the man many called "the wisest American." Ben had a wonderful time. It made him proud to hear so much praise. Besides, he always did enjoy a good party.

But he was glad when all the celebrations began to die down. "I intend to spend the rest of my life as a private man," he said.

But it was not to be—not yet. America still had one more job for Ben Franklin.

The separate states were not getting along

very well. Many of them were printing their own money. They were making laws that other states didn't like. They were even trying to tax one another. They were beginning, in fact, to act like separate countries instead of the one nation Ben and the others had fought so hard to create. The leading men of the new United States knew that something must be done—and quickly. In 1787 they met in Philadelphia to work out a plan for a new central government that would be stronger than any one state.

Benjamin Franklin was asked to be a member of this Constitutional Convention. Once more he accepted what he felt was his duty. He was eighty-one now, the oldest man there by twenty years. He was not well, and sometimes he took catnaps when the others argued over details. He never missed a meeting, and he was there to sign the document that Americans still live by—the United States Constitution.

Benjamin Franklin was the only *one* of the Founding Fathers to sign all *four* of the major documents that made the United States of America possible:

The Declaration of Independence
The wartime treaty with France
The peace treaty with England
The Constitution of the United States of America.

For years Ben had made light remarks about growing old. "When I consider how many terrible diseases the human body is liable to, I comfort myself that only three have fallen my share: the gout, the stone, and old age."

In the late 1780s life, however, was slowing down for him. He was crippled by gout, and his kidney stones hurt so much that sometimes he could not get out of bed for weeks at a time. But he refused to give in to any of it. He simply held court from his bed, reading, writing long letters, laughing, playing chess, and enjoying the visits of friends.

A great joy for Ben during those last years were his many grandchildren. "I have seven promising ones by my daughter Sally alone," he wrote a friend. The littlest was only five months old—"a little good-natured girl whom I begin to love as well as the rest."

Ben wasn't able to get out of bed much.

But he had not, as a friend said, "lost any of his wit or ability to think." There was something else he kept until the very end—his ability to care about people.

The Declaration of Independence said, "All men are created equal . . ." But what about slaves? These black Americans were not considered equal at all. And this bothered Ben a lot. His last public act was to sign a petition to the first Congress of the United States calling for the end of slavery.

In this, as in so many other things, he was far ahead of his times. The institution of slavery would continue to haunt the United States for almost another hundred years.

A few months later, on April 17, 1790, with his favorite grandsons, Temple and Benny, by his bedside, Benjamin Franklin died.

More than twenty thousand people gathered to walk behind his coffin. They came to honor him for his achievements—as a businessman, printer, scientist, inventor, diplomat, and statesman. They came to show their love for the man he had been—wise, witty, funny, kind, generous, and caring.

Highlights in the Life of
BENJAMIN FRANKLIN

1706   On January 17 Benjamin Franklin is born on Milk Street in Boston, in the colony of Massachusetts.

1718   Benjamin Franklin is apprenticed without pay to his brother James.

1722   Ben writes a series of articles called the Silence Dogood Letters for the *New England Courant.*

1723   Ben quarrels with James and flees to Philadelphia, Pennsylvania.

1728   Ben, with a partner, opens a new print shop in Philadelphia.

1729   On October 2 Ben begins to publish a highly successful newspaper called the *Pennsylvania Gazette.*

1730   Ben marries Deborah Read. They soon have a son named William.

1731   Ben plans and starts the first public library in America.

1732 In October Ben's second son, Francis, is born.

In December, Ben publishes the first edition of *Poor Richard's Almanac*.

1736 Ben organizes the first volunteer fire brigade in Philadelphia.

Four-year-old Francis dies of small-pox.

1737 Ben is appointed postmaster of Philadelphia.

1742 Ben invents the Franklin Stove.

1743 In May Ben proposes that men of learning and science unite to form the American Philosophical Society, which still exists today.

In September a daughter named Sarah, or Sally, is born to Ben and Debbie Franklin.

1751 Ben is elected to the Pennsylvania Assembly, the local governing body for the colony.

1752 In June Ben performs his dangerous electrical experiment of drawing lightning down from a storm cloud with a metal key tied to a kite.

1753   Ben invents the lightning rod.
Ben is appointed deputy postmaster general for the northern colonies.

1757   In March Ben sails for England to represent many of the colonies with their growing grievances against the mother country.

1766   Ben fights hard in England to get the Stamp Act repealed.

1771   In August Ben begins *The Autobiography of Benjamin Franklin.*

1774   In December Ben's wife Debbie dies in Philadelphia.
On April 19, while Ben is at sea, the first shots of the Revolutionary War are fired in Lexington, Massachusetts.
On May 6 Ben is appointed to the Second Continental Congress.

1776   On June 10 Ben is picked to sit on the committee to draw up the Declaration of Independence.
Ben is asked to go to France and seek money and supplies to help support the revolution.

1778   Ben works hard to convince the French government to sign a treaty of alliance with the United States.

1781   The Revolutionary War ends.

1783   Ben helps draw up the treaty of peace between the United States and England.

1784   Ben invents bifocals.

1785   Ben returns to America and is given a hero's welcome.

1787   Ben, at eighty-one, is the oldest man to sign the United States Constitution.

1789   Ben signs a petition to the first Congress of the United States calling for an end to slavery.

        On April 17 Benjamin Franklin dies.